Cascading

I0013045

Cascading Style Sheets at a first glance
BOOK 1: Redefining to enhance front-end website

Table of Contents

a) Introduction to CSS
b) CSS Roadmap
c) CSS Syntax and Structure
d) CSS Selectors and Specificity
e) Including CSS in Your Web Pages
f) Measurement Units in CSS
g) Working with Colors in CSS
h) Backgrounds in CSS
i) Typography in CSS
j) Text Styling in CSS
k) Working with Images in CSS
l) Styling Links with CSS
m) CSS Tables and Layouts
n) Borders and Outlines in CSS
o) Advanced Border Properties
p) Margins and Spacing in CSS
q) CSS Mastery Challenge

Learning Objectives:

By the end of this course, learners will be able to:

1. Introduction to CSS
- Explain what CSS is and its role in web development.
- Describe the advantages of using CSS over inline styling.

2. CSS Roadmap
- Understand the evolution of CSS and its different versions.
- Identify key CSS features and how they improve web design.

3. CSS Syntax and Structure
- Write basic CSS rules, including selectors, properties, and values.
- Understand how CSS declaration blocks work.

4. CSS Selectors and Specificity

- Use different types of CSS selectors effectively.
- Explain CSS specificity and how it affects style application.

5. Including CSS in Your Web Pages
- Apply CSS using inline, internal, and external styles.
- Link external CSS files correctly.

6. Measurement Units in CSS
- Differentiate between absolute and relative units.
- Use appropriate units for responsive web design.

7. Working with Colors in CSS
- Apply colors using HEX, RGB, and HSL formats.
- Implement transparency and opacity in designs.

8. Backgrounds in CSS
- Set background colors, images, and gradients.
- Adjust background positioning, size, and repeat properties.

9. Typography in CSS
- Customize fonts using font-family, size, weight, and style.
- Use @font-face to include custom fonts.

10. Text Styling in CSS
- Format text using alignment, decoration, transform, and shadow properties.
- Control line height and spacing for readability.

11. Working with Images in CSS
- Set image dimensions and positioning.
- Apply filters and effects to images using CSS.

12. Styling Links with CSS
- Customize link styles using pseudo-classes (hover, active, visited).
- Design interactive link effects.

13. CSS Tables and Layouts
- Style tables using border, padding, and alignment properties.
- Make tables responsive for different screen sizes.

14. Borders and Outlines in CSS
- Apply and customize border styles, thickness, and colors.
- Implement border-radius for rounded effects.

15. Advanced Border Properties
- Use border-block and border-inline for logical properties.
- Create multi-border effects and advanced designs.

16. Margins and Spacing in CSS
- Control layout spacing using margin and padding properties.
- Explain the concept of margin collapsing.

17. Practice Exercises
- Apply learned CSS concepts to real-world web design scenarios.
- Debug and optimize CSS code for better performance.

A. Introduction to CSS

Overview of Cascading Style Sheets (CSS)

What is CSS?

CSS (Cascading Style Sheets) is a stylesheet language used to control the appearance of web pages. It allows developers to separate content (HTML) from design, making web pages visually appealing and easier to maintain.

Key Features of CSS:

- Controls colors, fonts, spacing, and layout
- Enhances the user experience (UX)
- Enables responsive web design for different screen sizes
- Allows reusability and consistency across multiple web pages

Example: CSS in Action

Let's say we have an HTML paragraph:

<p>This is a simple paragraph.</p>

By default, this text appears in the browser's default font and size. We can use CSS to style it:

```
p {
    color: blue;
    font-size: 20px;
    font-family: Arial, sans-serif;
}
```

This will change the paragraph's text to blue, 20px in size, and in Arial font.

Importance and Role of CSS in Web Development

Why is CSS Important?

Without CSS, web pages would look plain and unstructured. CSS enhances websites by:

- Improving Visual Appeal – Customizing colors, fonts, and layouts
- Making Websites Responsive – Ensuring content looks good on all devices
- Increasing Maintainability – Changing styles in one place updates the entire website
- Enhancing User Experience – Providing interactive and engaging designs

Example: How CSS Improves Web Design

Imagine a webpage without CSS:

```
<h1>Welcome to My Website</h1>
<p>This is a basic webpage without styling.</p>
```

The result: The text will appear as plain black text on a white background.

Now, let's add some CSS to improve it:

```
body {
    background-color: lightgray;
    text-align: center;
    font-family: Verdana, sans-serif;
}

h1 {
    color: darkblue;
}
```

```
p {
    font-size: 18px;
    color: darkgreen;
}
```

The result: The webpage now has a gray background, centered text, and customized colors and fonts.

Practice Lab: Getting Started with CSS

Goal: Create a simple HTML page and apply basic CSS styles.

Steps:

1. Create an HTML File

- Open a text editor (e.g., VS Code, Notepad++).
- Save a new file as index.html.
- Add the following code:

```
<!DOCTYPE html>
<html lang="en">
<head>
    <meta charset="UTF-8">
    <meta name="viewport" content="width=device-width, initial-scale=1.0">
    <title>My First CSS Page</title>
    <link rel="stylesheet" href="styles.css">
</head>
<body>
    <h1>Welcome to My First Styled Webpage</h1>
    <p>This is my first webpage with CSS.</p>
</body>
</html>
```

2. Create a CSS File

- Save a new file as styles.css in the same folder.
- Add the following styles:

```css
body {
    background-color: #f0f8ff;
    text-align: center;
    font-family: Arial, sans-serif;
}

h1 {
    color: #ff4500;
}

p {
    color: #008000;
    font-size: 20px;
}
```

3. Open index.html in a Web Browser

- Right-click the file and select Open with > Chrome/Edge/Firefox.
- Observe the applied styles!

B. CSS Roadmap

Understanding the Evolution of CSS

What is the Evolution of CSS?
CSS has evolved over the years to introduce better styling capabilities, making websites more interactive and responsive. When the web started, HTML was mainly used for structure, and CSS was later introduced to separate design from content.

Key Milestones in CSS Evolution

- CSS1 (1996) – Introduced basic styling (colors, fonts, margins, borders)
- CSS2 (1998) – Added better layout control (positioning, media types)
- CSS2.1 (2004) – Improved compatibility and fixed issues in CSS2
- CSS3 (2011 - Present) – Introduced advanced features like animations, gradients, Flexbox, Grid, and media queries

Example: How CSS Evolution Improves Styling
Let's see how CSS has improved with a simple example.

CSS1 Approach (Basic Styling)
```
h1 {
    color: blue;
    font-size: 20px;
}
```
Only allows simple color and font size changes.

CSS3 Approach (Advanced Features)
```
h1 {
    color: blue;
    font-size: 20px;
    text-shadow: 2px 2px 5px gray;
```

7

```
transition: color 0.5s ease-in-out;
}

h1:hover {
    color: red;
}
```

Enhancements with CSS3:

- Text Shadows
- Smooth Transitions
- Hover Effects

CSS Versions and Specifications

What are CSS Versions?
Each version of CSS adds new capabilities and improvements.

CSS Version	Year Released	Key Features
CSS1	1996	Basic styling (colors, fonts, borders)
CSS2	1998	Positioning, z-index, media types
CSS2.1	2004	Bug fixes, improved stability
CSS3	2011-Present	Animations, Gradients, Flexbox, Grid, Responsive Design

Example: Comparing CSS2 vs. CSS3 Layout Techniques

CSS2 (Table-Based Layout)
```
table {
    width: 100%;
    border-collapse: collapse;
}
```

Websites relied on tables for layouts (not flexible).

CSS3 (Flexbox for Layout)
```
.container {
    display: flex;
    justify-content: space-between;
}
```

More efficient, responsive, and flexible layouts with CSS3!

Practice Lab: CSS Roadmap in Action
Goal: Understand the improvements in CSS versions through hands-on practice.
Steps:
1. Create an HTML File (index.html)

```
<!DOCTYPE html>
<html lang="en">
<head>
    <meta charset="UTF-8">
    <meta name="viewport" content="width=device-width, initial-scale=1.0">
    <title>CSS Evolution</title>
    <link rel="stylesheet" href="styles.css">
</head>
<body>
    <h1>CSS Roadmap Example</h1>
    <p>Hover over the text to see CSS3 effects in action!</p>
</body>
</html>
```

2. Create a CSS File (styles.css)

```
body {
    text-align: center;
    font-family: Arial, sans-serif;
}

h1 {
    color: blue;
    font-size: 30px;
    text-shadow: 3px 3px 5px gray;
    transition: color 0.5s ease-in-out;
}

h1:hover {
    color: red;
}

p {
    font-size: 20px;
    color: darkgreen;
}
```

3. Open index.html in a Web Browser
- Observe how the text changes when hovered!
- Compare older CSS techniques with modern approaches.

With this roadmap, you now understand how CSS has evolved and why CSS3 is powerful!

C. CSS Syntax and Structure

CSS Syntax and Structure

CSS (Cascading Style Sheets) is a rule-based language that defines how HTML elements should be displayed. It consists of selectors, properties, and values that together control the styling of web pages.

Basic CSS Rules and Properties

CSS Syntax Breakdown

A CSS rule consists of:

- Selector – Targets the HTML element(s) to be styled
- Property – Defines what aspect of the element to style (color, font, size, etc.)
- Value – Specifies the setting for the property

```
selector {
    property: value;
}
```

Example: Basic CSS Rule

```
p {
    color: blue;
    font-size: 20px;
}
```

This rule applies to all <p> elements, setting the text color to blue and font size to 20px.

Miquill Nyle

Common CSS Properties

Property	Description	Example
color	Changes text color	color: red;
font-size	Adjusts text size	font-size: 16px;
background	Sets background color/image	background: yellow;
margin	Adds space outside elements	margin: 10px;
padding	Adds space inside elements	padding: 15px;

CSS Declaration Blocks and Selectors

What is a Declaration Block?

A declaration block contains multiple property-value pairs inside curly braces {}.

Example:

h1 {

   color: green;

   text-align: center;

   font-family: Arial, sans-serif;

}

Explanation:

All <h1> elements will be green, centered, and use Arial font.

CSS Selectors: Targeting Elements

Selectors are used to apply styles to specific HTML elements.

1. Element Selector (Targets specific elements)

h1 {

```
    color: blue;
}
```

Applies to all <h1> elements.

2. Class Selector (Reusable styling for multiple elements)
```
.title {
    font-size: 24px;
    color: darkred;
}
```

Applied using class="title" in HTML.
<p class="title">This is a styled paragraph.</p>

3. ID Selector (Unique styling for one element)
```
#header {
    background-color: lightgray;
}
```

Applied using id="header" in HTML.
<div id="header">Welcome to My Website</div>

4. Grouping Selector (Applies styles to multiple elements)
```
h1, h2, p {
    font-family: Arial, sans-serif;
}
```

Styles <h1>, <h2>, and <p> at the same time.

Practice Lab: Writing CSS Syntax and Selectors

Goal: Create a webpage and style different elements using CSS selectors.

Steps:

1. Create an HTML File (index.html)

```
<!DOCTYPE html>
<html lang="en">
<head>
    <meta charset="UTF-8">
    <meta name="viewport" content="width=device-width, initial-scale=1.0">
    <title>CSS Syntax Example</title>
    <link rel="stylesheet" href="styles.css">
</head><body>
    <h1>Welcome to CSS Styling</h1>
    <p class="title">This is a paragraph with a class selector.</p>
    <div id="header">This div has an ID selector.</div>
</body></html>
```

Create a CSS File (styles.css)

```
/* Element Selector */
h1 {
    color: blue;
    text-align: center;
}
/* Class Selector */
.title {
    font-size: 20px;
    color: darkred;
}

/* ID Selector */
```

```
#header {
    background-color: lightgray;
    padding: 10px;
    text-align: center;
}
```

3. Open index.html in a Web Browser
Observe how different selectors apply styles!

This guide introduces CSS syntax, declaration blocks, and selectors.

D. CSS Selectors and Specificity

What is CSS Selectors and Specificity?
CSS selectors allow you to target specific HTML elements and apply styles to them. However, when multiple rules apply to the same element, CSS specificity and the cascade determine which styles take priority.

Types of Selectors: Element, Class, ID, Attribute, Pseudo-Classes
1. Element Selector
Targets all elements of a specific type.

Example:
```
p {
    color: blue;
}
```
Applies to: All <p> elements.

2. Class Selector (.)
Targets multiple elements with the same class.

Example:
```
.highlight {
    background-color: yellow;
}
```

HTML Usage:
```
<p class="highlight">This text has a yellow background.</p>
```

Best for: Reusable styles across multiple elements.

3. ID Selector (#)

Targets a unique element by its ID.

Example:

#main-header {

   font-size: 24px;

}

HTML Usage: <h1 id="main-header">Welcome!</h1>

Note: ID selectors have higher specificity than class selectors.

4. Attribute Selector ([])

Targets elements based on attributes (e.g., href, type).

Example:

input[type="text"] {

   border: 2px solid black;

}

Applies to:

<input type="text" placeholder="Enter name">

<input type="password">

Best for: Styling form elements.

5. Pseudo-Class Selector (:)

Targets elements in specific states (hover, focus, first-child, etc.).

Example: Hover Effect
button:hover {
  background-color: green;
  color: white;
}

Applies to: <button>Hover me!</button>
Best for: Adding interactivity.

Understanding Specificity and the Cascade

When multiple CSS rules apply to the same element, specificity and the cascade determine which rule wins.

CSS Specificity Formula:
1. Inline styles (style="color: red;") → Highest priority
2. ID selectors (#header) → High priority
3. Class, attribute, and pseudo-class selectors (.title, [type="text"], :hover)
4. Element selectors (h1, p) → Lowest priority

Example: Conflicting Rules
p {
  color: blue;
} /* Element Selector */

.special {
  color: green;
} /* Class Selector (Higher Specificity) */

```
#unique {
    color: red;
} /* ID Selector (Highest Specificity) */
```

HTML Usage:

```
<p class="special" id="unique">What color am I?</p>
```

Result: Text will be red because the ID selector has the highest specificity.

Practice Lab: Playing with Selectors and Specificity

Goal: Create a webpage to test different selectors and CSS specificity.

Steps:

1. Create an HTML File (index.html)

```
<!DOCTYPE html>
<html lang="en">
<head>
    <meta charset="UTF-8">
    <meta name="viewport" content="width=device-width, initial-scale=1.0">
    <title>CSS Selectors & Specificity</title>
    <link rel="stylesheet" href="styles.css">
</head>
<body>

    <h1 id="main-header">Welcome to CSS Selectors</h1>

    <p class="special">This is a paragraph with a class selector.</p>
```

```
<p id="unique">This paragraph has an ID selector.</p>

<button>Hover over me!</button>

<input type="text" placeholder="Type here...">

</body>
</html>
```

2. Create a CSS File (styles.css)

```css
/* Element Selector */
p {
    color: blue;
}

/* Class Selector */
.special {
    color: green;
}

/* ID Selector */
#unique {
    color: red;
}

/* Attribute Selector */
input[type="text"] {
    border: 2px solid black;
}
```

```
/* Pseudo-Class Selector */
button:hover {
    background-color: green;
    color: white;
}
```

3. Open index.html in a Web Browser

Test how selectors and specificity affect the styling!

Now you understand how CSS selectors and specificity control web styling!

E. Including CSS in Your Web Pages

CSS (Cascading Style Sheets) can be included in a webpage using different methods: Inline CSS, Internal CSS, and External CSS. Each method has its own use case and advantages.

Inline, Internal, and External Stylesheets

1. Inline CSS
Definition: Inline CSS applies styles directly to a specific HTML element using the style attribute.

Example:
This is an inline-styled paragraph.

Best for: Quick, one-time styling.
Drawback: Hard to maintain if applied to multiple elements.

2. Internal CSS (Within <style> Tag)
Definition: Internal CSS is written inside a <style> block in the <head> section of the HTML document.

Example:
```
<!DOCTYPE html>
<html lang="en">
<head>
  <meta charset="UTF-8">
  <meta name="viewport" content="width=device-width, initial-scale=1.0">
  <title>Internal CSS Example</title>
```

```
<style>
  p {
      color: blue;
      font-size: 18px;
  }
  </style>
</head>
<body>
  <p>This paragraph is styled using internal CSS.</p>
</body>
</html>
```

Best for: Small projects or single-page styles.

Drawback: Not reusable across multiple pages.

3. External CSS (Separate .css File)

Definition: External CSS stores styles in a separate .css file and links it to the HTML file using <link>.

Example:

Step 1: Create an external CSS file (styles.css).

```
p {
   color: green;
   font-size: 18px;
}
```

Step 2: Link it in the HTML file (index.html).

```
<!DOCTYPE html>
<html lang="en">
```

```
<head>
  <meta charset="UTF-8">
  <meta name="viewport" content="width=device-width, initial-scale=1.0">
  <title>External CSS Example</title>
  <link rel="stylesheet" href="styles.css">
</head>
<body>
  <p>This paragraph is styled using an external CSS file.</p>
</body>
</html>
```

Best for: Large projects, reusable styles, and clean code.

Drawback: Requires an additional file.

Linking External CSS Files

To use an external stylesheet, add the following inside the <head> of the HTML file: <link rel="stylesheet" href="styles.css">

Key Attributes:

- rel="stylesheet" → Specifies that the file is a stylesheet.
- href="styles.css" → Specifies the file location.

Practice Lab: Testing Different CSS Inclusion Methods

Goal: Understand the difference between inline, internal, and external CSS.

Steps:

1. Create an HTML File (index.html)

```
<!DOCTYPE html>
<html lang="en">
<head>
  <meta charset="UTF-8">
  <meta name="viewport" content="width=device-width, initial-scale=1.0">
  <title>CSS Inclusion Methods</title>

  <!-- Internal CSS -->
  <style>
    h1 {
        color: blue;
        text-align: center;
    }
  </style>

  <!-- External CSS -->
  <link rel="stylesheet" href="styles.css">
</head>
<body>

  <!-- Inline CSS -->
  <p style="color: red;">This paragraph uses inline CSS.</p>

  <h1>This heading uses internal CSS.</h1>
```

```
<p>This paragraph will be styled using external CSS.</p>

</body>
</html>
```

2. Create a CSS File (styles.css)

```
p {
    color: green;
    font-size: 18px;
    text-align: center;
}
```

3. Open index.html in a Web Browser

Observe how inline, internal, and external CSS styles are applied!

Now you understand the different ways to include CSS in web pages!

F. Measurement Units in CSS

What is Measurement Units in CSS?

CSS uses measurement units to define sizes for elements such as text, margins, padding, width, and height. These units can be categorized into absolute units and relative units.

Absolute Units: Pixels, Points, Inches

Absolute units have fixed values and do not change based on the surrounding elements or screen size. They are useful when you need precise control over element sizes.

Unit	Description	Example
px (Pixels)	Smallest unit of display, relative to screen resolution	width: 200px;
pt (Points)	Used in print. 1 pt = 1/72 of an inch	font-size: 12pt;
in (Inches)	1 inch = 2.54 cm	width: 2in;

Example: Absolute Units

```
.box {
    width: 300px;
    height: 100px;
    font-size: 16pt;
    border: 2in solid black;
}
```

Best for: Print styling or when precise sizing is required.

Drawback: Not responsive on different screen sizes.

Relative Units: EM, REM, %, VW, VH

Relative units adjust dynamically based on the size of other elements or the viewport. These are ideal for responsive designs.

Unit	Relative To	Example
em	Parent element's font size	font-size: 2em; (2× parent size)
rem	Root <html> font size	font-size: 1.5rem;
%	Parent element's size	width: 50%; (Half of parent width)
vw	1% of viewport width	width: 50vw; (Half of screen width)
vh	1% of viewport height	height: 100vh; (Full screen height)

Example: Relative Units

.container {

   width: 80%;

   font-size: 1.5rem;

}

.box {

   width: 50vw;

   height: 30vh;

}

Best for: Responsive layouts that adapt to different screen sizes.

Drawback: Can be tricky to predict exact sizes.

Practice Lab: Using Measurement Units

Goal: Experiment with different measurement units to understand how they affect elements.

Steps:

1. Create an HTML File (index.html)

```
<!DOCTYPE html>
<html lang="en">
<head>
    <meta charset="UTF-8">
    <meta name="viewport" content="width=device-width, initial-scale=1.0">
    <title>CSS Measurement Units</title>
    <link rel="stylesheet" href="styles.css">
</head>
<body>

    <h1>CSS Measurement Units</h1>

    <div class="absolute-box">Absolute Units (300px × 100px)</div>

    <div class="relative-box">Relative Units (Width: 50%)</div>

    <div class="viewport-box">Viewport Units (50vw × 30vh)</div>

</body>
</html>
```

2. Create a CSS File (styles.css)

```
h1 {
    font-size: 2rem; /* Root-relative */
```

```
    text-align: center;
}

/* Absolute unit */
.absolute-box {
    width: 300px;
    height: 100px;
    background-color: lightblue;
    margin: 10px;
}

/* Relative unit */
.relative-box {
    width: 50%;
    background-color: lightgreen;
    padding: 20px;
}

/* Viewport unit */
.viewport-box {
    width: 50vw;
    height: 30vh;
    background-color: lightcoral;
}
```

3. Open index.html in a Web Browser

Test how different measurement units affect element sizes!

Now you understand absolute and relative units in CSS!

G. Working with Colors in CSS

What is working with Colors in CSS?

CSS allows you to define colors using different methods such as named colors, RGB, HEX, and HSL. You can also control transparency and opacity to create visually appealing designs.

Color Naming, RGB, HEX, HSL

1. Named Colors

CSS provides 147 predefined color names like red, blue, green, etc.

Example:

```
h1 {
    color: red;
}
```

2. RGB (Red, Green, Blue) Format

The RGB model defines colors using red (R), green (G), and blue (B) values ranging from 0 to 255.

```
Example:
p {
    color: rgb(255, 0, 0); /* Pure Red */
}
```

Best for: When you need precise color control.

3. HEX (Hexadecimal) Format

Hex codes are six-digit color codes that represent RGB values in base-16 (#RRGGBB).

Example:

div {
  background-color: #00ff00; /* Pure Green */
}

Best for: Compact and widely used in web development.

4. HSL (Hue, Saturation, Lightness) Format

- Hue (H): Color type (0° to 360°)
- Saturation (S): Intensity (0% to 100%)
- Lightness (L): Brightness (0% to 100%)

Example:

button {
  background-color: hsl(240, 100%, 50%); /* Pure Blue */
}

Best for: Creating shades and tints easily.

Transparency and Opacity in CSS

1. Opacity Property

The opacity property controls the transparency of an element (values range from 0 (fully transparent) to 1 (fully visible)).

Example:

.transparent-box {

   background-color: blue;

   opacity: 0.5;

}

Making elements semi-transparent.

2. RGBA (RGB + Alpha)

The a in rgba() represents alpha transparency (0 to 1).

Example:

button {

   background-color: hsla(120, 100%, 50%, 0.3); /* Light Green with 30% opacity

*/

}

Best for: Creating smooth transparency effects.

Practice Lab: Experimenting with Colors and Transparency

Goal: Understand how different color formats and opacity work in CSS.

Steps:

1. Create an HTML File (index.html)

<!DOCTYPE html>

<html lang="en">

<head>

   <meta charset="UTF-8">

   <meta name="viewport" content="width=device-width, initial-scale=1.0">

   <title>CSS Colors and Transparency</title>

```
    <link rel="stylesheet" href="styles.css">
</head>
<body>

    <h1>CSS Colors and Transparency</h1>

    <div class="color-box color-name">Named Color (Blue)</div>
    <div class="color-box color-rgb">RGB Color (255, 165, 0)</div>
    <div class="color-box color-hex">HEX Color (#ff00ff)</div>
    <div class="color-box color-hsl">HSL Color (200, 100%, 50%)</div>

    <div class="color-box transparent">50% Transparent Box</div>

</body>
</html>
```

2. Create a CSS File (styles.css)
```
body {
    text-align: center;
    font-family: Arial, sans-serif;
}

/* Named Color */
.color-name {
    background-color: blue;
}

/* RGB Color */
.color-rgb {
```

```
    background-color: rgb(255, 165, 0); /* Orange */
}

/* HEX Color */
.color-hex {
    background-color: #ff00ff; /* Magenta */
}

/* HSL Color */
.color-hsl {
    background-color: hsl(200, 100%, 50%); /* Cyan */
}

/* Transparent Box */
.transparent {
    background-color: rgba(0, 0, 0, 0.5); /* Semi-transparent Black */
}

/* Styling for color boxes */
.color-box {
    width: 200px;
    height: 50px;
    margin: 10px auto;
    color: white;
    line-height: 50px;
}
```

3. Open index.html in a Web Browser

Observe how different colors and transparency levels work!

Summary

Feature	Description	Example
Named Colors	Predefined CSS colors	`color: blue;`
RGB	Defines colors using Red. Green. and Blue	`color: rgb(255, 0, 0);`
HEX	Six-digit hexadecimal representation of RGB	`color: #ff5733;`
HSL	Uses Hue. Saturation. and Lightness	`color: hsl(240, 100%, 50%);`
Opacity	Controls element transparency	`opacity: 0.5;`
RGBA	Adds transparency to RGB	`background-color: rgba(255, 0, 0, 0.5);`
HSLA	Adds transparency to HSL	`background-color: hsla(120, 100%, 50%, 0.3);`

Now you understand color formats and transparency in CSS!

H. Backgrounds in CSS

What is Backgrounds in CSS?

Backgrounds in CSS allow us to customize the appearance of web pages by adding solid colors, images, gradients, and patterns. We can control the size, position, and repeat behavior of background elements to create visually appealing designs.

Background Color and Images

1. Background Color
The background-color property sets the background color of an element.

Example:
```
body {
    background-color: lightblue; /* Light blue background */
}
```

Best for: Simple designs and easy readability.

2. Background Images
The background-image property allows us to use images as backgrounds.

Example:
```
body {
    background-image: url('background.jpg'); /* Set an image as background */
}
```

Best for: Decorative effects, branding, and visual storytelling.
Drawback: Large images can slow down page loading.

Background Size, Position, and Repeat

1. Background Size
The background-size property controls how the background image is displayed.

Value	Description
auto	Default size (actual image size)
cover	Scales the image to cover the entire element
contain	Scales the image to fit within the element
100px 200px	Custom width and height

Example:
```
body {
    background-image: url('background.jpg');
    background-size: cover; /* Cover the entire page */
}
```

Best for: Making backgrounds look good on different screen sizes.

2. Background Position
The background-position property defines where the background image appears.

Value	Description
left top	Aligns to the top-left corner
center center	Centers the image
right bottom	Aligns to the bottom-right corner
50% 50%	Centers using percentage

Example:
```
body {
    background-image: url('background.jpg');
    background-position: center center;
}
```

Best for: Aligning background images for better visual appeal.

3. Background Repeat
The background-repeat property defines if the background image repeats or stays fixed.

Value	Description
repeat	Default: repeats the image both horizontally and vertically
no-repeat	Prevents the image from repeating
repeat-x	Repeats only horizontally
repeat-y	Repeats only vertically

Example:
body {
   background-image: url('pattern.png');
   background-repeat: repeat-x; /* Repeat horizontally */
}

Best for: Patterns and textures.

Practice Lab: Experimenting with CSS Backgrounds
Goal: Learn how background properties work in CSS.
Steps:
1. Create an HTML File (index.html)
<!DOCTYPE html>
<html lang="en">
<head>
  <meta charset="UTF-8">
  <meta name="viewport" content="width=device-width, initial-scale=1.0">
  <title>CSS Backgrounds</title>
  <link rel="stylesheet" href="styles.css">
</head>
<body>

  <h1>CSS Background Properties</h1>

  <div class="box background-color">Solid Background Color</div>
  <div class="box background-image">Background Image</div>
  <div class="box background-size">Background Size: Cover</div>
  <div class="box background-position">Background Position: Center</div>
  <div class="box background-repeat">Background Repeat: No-Repeat</div>

</body>
</html>

2. Create a CSS File (styles.css)

39

```
body {
    text-align: center;
    font-family: Arial, sans-serif;
    background-color: lightgray; /* Page background */
}

.box {
    width: 300px;
    height: 100px;
    margin: 20px auto;
    padding: 20px;
    color: white;
    font-size: 18px;
    line-height: 100px;
    text-align: center;
    border-radius: 10px;
}

/* Solid Background */
.background-color {
    background-color: steelblue;
}

/* Background Image */
.background-image {
    background-image: url('background.jpg');
    background-size: cover;
}

/* Background Size */
.background-size {
    background-image: url('background.jpg');
    background-size: contain;
}

/* Background Position */
.background-position {
    background-image: url('background.jpg');
    background-position: center;
    background-size: cover;
}

/* Background Repeat */
```

```
.background-repeat {
    background-image: url('pattern.png');
    background-repeat: no-repeat;
    background-size: cover;
}
```

3. Open index.html in a Web Browser
Observe how different background properties affect the appearance of elements!

Summary

Property	Description	Example
background-color	Sets background color	background-color: red;
background-image	Adds a background image	background-image: url('bg.jpg');
background-size	Defines image scaling	background-size: cover;
background-position	Positions the image	background-position: center;
background-repeat	Defines repeat behavior	background-repeat: no-repeat;

I. <u>Typography in CSS</u>

What is a Typography in CSS?

Typography is a crucial aspect of web design that enhances readability, aesthetics, and user experience. CSS provides several properties to control fonts, including font-family, font-size, font-weight, and font-style. You can also use the @font-face rule to include custom fonts in your project.

Customizing Fonts Using Font-Family, Size, Weight, and Style

1. Font-Family

The font-family property defines the font used for text.

- You can list multiple fonts as fallback options (in case a font is unavailable).
- Some common font categories:
  - Serif (e.g., Times New Roman) → Traditional & formal
  - Sans-serif (e.g., Arial) → Clean & modern
  - Monospace (e.g., Courier New) → Used for coding

Example:

```
p {
    font-family: Arial, Helvetica, sans-serif;
}
```

Best for: Setting the primary font for a webpage.

Tip: Always include a generic font family (e.g., sans-serif) as a fallback.

2. font-size: Adjusting Text Size

The font-size property controls the size of the text.

- Can be set in pixels (px), em, rem, percentage (%), or viewport units (vw, vh).

Example:

h1 {

    font-size: 32px;

}

p {

    font-size: 1.2em; /* Relative to parent element */

}

Best for: Making text readable across different devices.

Tip: Using em and rem ensures scalability for responsive designs.

3. font-weight: Making Text Bold or Light

The font-weight property defines the thickness of text.

Value	Description
normal	Default thickness
bold	Bold text
lighter	Lighter than normal
100 - 900	Numeric values (higher = bolder)

Example:

h2 {

    font-weight: bold;

}

p {

    font-weight: 300; /* Light font */

}

Best for: Highlighting headings and important text.

4. font-style: Italicizing Text

The font-style property allows text to be italicized.

Value	Description
normal	Default (non-italic)
italic	Italic text
oblique	Slightly slanted text

Example:

blockquote {

    font-style: italic;

}

Best for: Emphasizing quotes or special text.

Use @font-face to Include Custom Fonts

By default, web browsers only support standard system fonts. To use custom fonts, we can import them using @font-face.

1. Using @font-face to Import Custom Fonts

Example:

@font-face {

    font-family: 'CustomFont';

    src: url('CustomFont.woff2') format('woff2'),

        url('CustomFont.woff') format('woff');

}

h1 {

    font-family: 'CustomFont', sans-serif;

}

Best for: Using unique fonts that are not installed on the user's device.

Tip: Use WOFF2 format for faster loading and better compatibility.

2. Importing Google Fonts

Google Fonts provides free web fonts that can be directly used in CSS.

Steps:

1. Visit Google Fonts
2. Select a font (e.g., Roboto)
3. Copy the <link> tag and paste it in your HTML <head>
4. Apply the font in CSS

Example:

<head>

  <link

href="https://fonts.googleapis.com/css2?family=Roboto:wght@400;700&display=swap" rel="stylesheet">

</head>

<style>

  body {

    font-family: 'Roboto', sans-serif;

  }

</style>

Best for: Quick and easy font integration.

Tip: Use display=swap to improve page loading speed.

Practice Lab: Experimenting with CSS Typography

Goal: Learn how to apply different fonts and styles using CSS.

1. Create an HTML File (index.html)

<!DOCTYPE html>

<html lang="en">

<head>

```
    <meta charset="UTF-8">
    <meta name="viewport" content="width=device-width, initial-scale=1.0">
    <title>CSS Typography</title>
    <link
href="https://fonts.googleapis.com/css2?family=Poppins:wght@300;600&display
=swap" rel="stylesheet">
    <link rel="stylesheet" href="styles.css">
</head>
<body>

    <h1>CSS Typography</h1>

    <p class="default-font">This is the default font.</p>
    <p class="custom-font">This text uses Google Fonts.</p>
    <p class="bold-text">This text is bold.</p>
    <p class="italic-text">This text is italicized.</p>

</body>
</html>
```

2. Create a CSS File (styles.css)

```
body {
    text-align: center;
    font-family: Arial, sans-serif;
}

/* Default Font */
.default-font {
    font-size: 18px;
```

```
}
/* Google Font */
.custom-font {
    font-family: 'Poppins', sans-serif;
    font-size: 20px;
}
/* Bold Text */
.bold-text {
    font-weight: bold;
}
/* Italic Text */
.italic-text {
    font-style: italic;
}
```

3. Open index.html in a Web Browser

Observe how different font properties affect the appearance of text!

Summary

Property	Description	Example
font-family	Defines the font type	font-family: Arial, sans-serif;
font-size	Sets the text size	font-size: 16px;
font-weight	Controls text thickness	font-weight: bold;
font-style	Defines italic/normal text	font-style: italic;
@font-face	Loads a custom font	@font-face { font-family: 'MyFont'; src: url('myfont.woff'); }
Google Fonts	Imports a font from Google	<link href="https://fonts.googleapis.com/css2?family=Poppins&display=swap">

J. Text Styling in CSS

What is Text Styling in CSS?

Text styling in CSS helps improve readability, aesthetics, and visual hierarchy on a webpage. You can control text alignment, spacing, decoration, transformations, and even add shadow effects for a more engaging design.

Text Alignment, Spacing, and Decoration

1. Text Alignment (text-align)

The text-align property defines the horizontal alignment of text within an element.

Value	Description
left	Aligns text to the left (default)
right	Aligns text to the right
center	Centers the text
justify	Stretches text so that it aligns both left and right

Example:

p {
    text-align: center; /* Centers text */
}

Best for: Centering titles or aligning body text for better readability.

2. Text Spacing (letter-spacing & line-height)

letter-spacing: Adjusts space between characters.

line-height: Controls the vertical space between lines of text.

Example:

```
p {
    letter-spacing: 2px; /* Increases space between letters */
    line-height: 1.5; /* Increases space between lines */
}
```

Best for: Making text more readable, especially for large paragraphs.

3. Text Decoration (text-decoration)

The text-decoration property is used to underline, overline, or strike through text.

Value	Description
none	No decoration
underline	Underlines text
overline	Adds a line above the text
line-through	Strikethrough effect

Example:

```
h1 {
    text-decoration: underline; /* Underlines the heading */
}
p {
    text-decoration: line-through; /* Strikethrough text */
}
```

Best for: Styling links and emphasizing headings.

Text Transform and Shadow Effects

1. Text Transform (text-transform)

The text-transform property changes the case of text.

Value	Description
uppercase	Converts text to ALL CAPS
lowercase	Converts text to lowercase
capitalize	Capitalizes the first letter of each word

Example:

h2 {

    text-transform: uppercase; /* Makes heading uppercase */

}

Best for: Ensuring consistent typography across your website.

2. Text Shadow (text-shadow)

The text-shadow property adds a shadow effect to text.

Syntax:

text-shadow: offsetX offsetY blurRadius color;

Example:

h1 {

    text-shadow: 2px 2px 5px gray; /* Adds a gray shadow */

}

Best for: Creating depth, emphasis, and stylistic effects in text.

Practice Lab: Experimenting with Text Styling

Goal: Learn how to control text alignment, spacing, decoration, transformation, and shadow effects in CSS.

Steps:

1. Create an HTML File (index.html)

```
<!DOCTYPE html>
<html lang="en">
<head>
    <meta charset="UTF-8">
    <meta name="viewport" content="width=device-width, initial-scale=1.0">
    <title>CSS Text Styling</title>
    <link rel="stylesheet" href="styles.css">
</head>
<body>

    <h1>Text Styling in CSS</h1>

    <p class="aligned-text">This text is centered.</p>
    <p class="spaced-text">This text has extra letter spacing and line height.</p>
    <p class="decorated-text">This text is underlined and has a line-through effect.</p>
    <p class="transformed-text">this text is capitalized.</p>
    <p class="shadow-text">This text has a shadow effect.</p>

</body>
</html>
```

2. Create a CSS File (styles.css)

```
body {
```

```css
    text-align: center;
    font-family: Arial, sans-serif;
}

/* Text Alignment */
.aligned-text {
    text-align: center;
}

/* Text Spacing */
.spaced-text {
    letter-spacing: 3px;
    line-height: 2;
}

/* Text Decoration */
.decorated-text {
    text-decoration: underline line-through;
}

/* Text Transform */
.transformed-text {
    text-transform: capitalize;
}

/* Text Shadow */
.shadow-text {
    text-shadow: 3px 3px 5px gray;
}
```

3. Open index.html in a Web Browser

Observe how different text properties affect the appearance of elements!

Summary

Property	Description	Example
text-align	Aligns text left, right, center, or justify	text-align: center;
letter-spacing	Adjusts space between letters	letter-spacing: 2px;
line-height	Adjusts space between lines	line-height: 1.5;
text-decoration	Adds underline, overline, or line-through	text-decoration: underline;
text-transform	Changes text case	text-transform: uppercase;
text-shadow	Adds shadow effect to text	text-shadow: 2px 2px 4px gray;

Miquill Nyle

J. <u>Working with Images in CSS</u>

What is working with Images in CSS?

Images are an essential part of web design, enhancing the visual appeal and user experience of a website. CSS allows you to control image dimensions, positioning, filters, and effects to create stunning designs.

Set Image Dimensions and Positioning

1. Controlling Image Size (width & height)
By default, images appear at their original size. However, you can resize those using CSS properties:

Property	Description
width	Sets the width of an image (in px, %, em, etc.)
height	Sets the height of an image
max-width	Ensures the image does not exceed a certain width

Example:

img {
   width: 300px; /* Set image width */
   height: auto; /* Keeps aspect ratio */
}

Best for: Ensuring images scale properly without distortion.
Tip: Use max-width: 100% to make images responsive!
Responsive Example:
img {

```
max-width: 100%;
height: auto;
}
```

Best for: Mobile-friendly layouts.

2. Positioning Images (float & object-fit)

A) Floating Images (float)

The float property helps position images within text.

Example:
```
img {
    float: right; /* Moves the image to the right */
    margin-left: 10px; /* Adds spacing */
}
```
Best for: Wrapping text around images.

B) Controlling Image Fit (object-fit)

When setting fixed dimensions, use object-fit to control how the image scales.

Value	Effect
cover	Fills the container while cropping the image
contain	Fits the entire image inside the container
none	Displays the original size

Example:
```
img {
    width: 300px;
    height: 200px;
    object-fit: cover; /* Image is cropped to fill the area */
}
```

Best for: Keeping a consistent image layout.

Apply Filters and Effects to Images Using CSS
CSS offers built-in filters to apply effects like blur, grayscale, brightness, and more.

1. CSS Filters for Image Effects
The filter property applies various effects:

Filter	Effect
blur(px)	Blurs the image
grayscale(%)	Converts image to black & white
brightness(%)	Adjusts brightness
contrast(%)	Adjusts contrast
sepia(%)	Adds a sepia (vintage) tone
invert(%)	Inverts colors

Example:
img {
   filter: grayscale(100%);
}
Best for: Converting an image to black & white.

Multiple Filters Example:
img {
   filter: brightness(120%) contrast(80%) sepia(50%);
}
Best for: Creating unique artistic effects.

2. Adding Hover Effects to Images

You can change an image filter when the user hovers over it.

Example:

img {

   transition: 0.5s; /* Smooth transition */

}

img:hover {

   filter: brightness(120%) blur(5px);

}

Best for: Interactive image hover effects.

Practice Lab: Experimenting with Image Styling

Goal: Learn how to resize, position, and apply filters to images using CSS.

Steps:

1. Create an HTML File (index.html)

<!DOCTYPE html>

<html lang="en">

<head>

   <meta charset="UTF-8">

   <meta name="viewport" content="width=device-width, initial-scale=1.0">

   <title>CSS Image Styling</title>

   <link rel="stylesheet" href="styles.css">

</head>

<body>

```
<h1>Working with Images in CSS</h1>

<h2>1. Resized Image</h2>
<img class="resized" src="image.jpg" alt="Resized Image">

<h2>2. Floating Image</h2>
<p>
    <img class="float-right" src="image.jpg" alt="Floating Image">
    This text wraps around the floating image.
</p>

<h2>3. Filtered Image</h2>
<img class="filtered" src="image.jpg" alt="Filtered Image">

<h2>4. Hover Effect</h2>
<img class="hover-effect" src="image.jpg" alt="Hover Effect Image">
```

```
</body>
</html>
```

2. Create a CSS File (styles.css)
```
/* Resizing Images */
.resized {
    width: 300px;
    height: auto;
}
/* Floating Image */
.float-right {
    float: right;
```

```
    width: 150px;
    margin-left: 10px;
}
/* Filtered Image */
.filtered {
    width: 300px;
    filter: sepia(60%);
}
/* Hover Effect */
.hover-effect {
    width: 300px;
    transition: 0.5s;
}
.hover-effect:hover {
    filter: brightness(120%) blur(3px);
}
```

3. Open index.html in a Web Browser

Observe how the images are styled differently!

Summary

Property	Description	Example
width & height	Controls image size	width: 300px; height: auto;
max-width	Makes images responsive	max-width: 100%;
float	Positions image left or right	float: right;
object-fit	Defines how images fit inside containers	object-fit: cover;
filter	Applies effects like blur, grayscale, brightness	filter: grayscale(100%);
transition	Smoothly animates changes	transition: 0.5s;

L. Styling Links with CSS

What is Styling Links with CSS?

Links (<a> tags) are crucial for web navigation. CSS allows you to customize their appearance and enhance user interaction using styles and pseudo-classes like hover, active, and visited.

Pseudo-Classes for Links (Hover, Active, Visited)

Understanding Link States
Links have different states that can be styled using CSS pseudo-classes:

Pseudo-Class	Description
:link	Styles a normal, unvisited link
:visited	Styles a visited link
:hover	Styles a link when mouse hovers over it
:active	Styles a link when it is clicked

Example: Basic Link Styling

```
a {
    color: blue;  /* Default link color */
    text-decoration: none; /* Removes underline */
}

a:visited {
    color: purple; /* Visited link color */
}
```

```
a:hover {
    color: red; /* Changes color on hover */
    text-decoration: underline; /* Adds underline */
}

a:active {
    color: orange; /* Changes color when clicked */
}
```

Best for: Creating visually distinct links that enhance usability.

Important Rule: The correct order for link states is:
a:link → a:visited → a:hover → a:active (LVHA order).

Customizing Link Appearance

1. Changing Font, Color, and Background
You can change the text color, add a background, and modify the font.

Example: Styled Button Link
```
a {
    display: inline-block; /* Makes the link behave like a button */
    padding: 10px 20px;
    background-color: #008CBA;
    color: white;
    text-decoration: none;
    border-radius: 5px;
}
```

```
a:hover {
    background-color: #005f73; /* Darker color on hover */
}
```

Best for: Creating button-like links.

2. Adding Icons to Links

You can add icons (e.g., ⚭, ▯) using CSS.

Example: Adding an External Link Icon

```
a::after {
    content: " ⚭"; /* Adds a link icon */
}
```

Best for: Indicating external links.

3. Styling Navigation Menus

CSS is often used to style navigation bars.

Example: Horizontal Navigation Bar

```
nav a {
    display: inline-block;
    padding: 10px 15px;
    color: white;
    background-color: #333;
    text-decoration: none;
}

nav a:hover {
    background-color: #555;
```

}

Best for: Creating beautiful navigation menus.

Practice Lab: Styling Links with CSS

Goal: Learn how to customize link appearance and use pseudo-classes.

Steps:

1. Create an HTML File (index.html)

```
<!DOCTYPE html>
<html lang="en">
<head>
   <meta charset="UTF-8">
   <meta name="viewport" content="width=device-width, initial-scale=1.0">
   <title>CSS Link Styling</title>
   <link rel="stylesheet" href="styles.css">
</head>
<body>

   <h1>Styling Links in CSS</h1>

   <h2>1. Basic Styled Link</h2>
   <a href="#">Visit My Website</a>

   <h2>2. Button-Style Link</h2>
   <a class="button" href="#">Click Me</a>

   <h2>3. Navigation Menu</h2>
   <nav>
      <a href="#">Home</a>
```

```
        <a href="#">About</a>
        <a href="#">Services</a>
        <a href="#">Contact</a>
    </nav>

</body>
</html>
```

2. Create a CSS File (styles.css)

```
/* Basic Link Styling */
a {
    color: blue;
    text-decoration: none;
}
a:visited {
    color: purple;
}
a:hover {
    color: red;
    text-decoration: underline;
}
a:active {
    color: orange;
}
/* Button-Style Link */
.button {
    display: inline-block;
    padding: 10px 20px;
    background-color: #008CBA;
```

```
    color: white;
    text-decoration: none;
    border-radius: 5px;
}

.button:hover {
    background-color: #005f73;
}
/* Navigation Menu */
nav a {
    display: inline-block;
    padding: 10px 15px;
    color: white;
    background-color: #333;
    text-decoration: none;
    margin: 5px;
}

nav a:hover {
    background-color: #555;
}
```

3. Open index.html in a Web Browser

Observe how links change in different states!

Summary

Property/Pseudo-Class	Description	Example
:link	Styles unvisited links	a:link { color: blue; }
:visited	Styles visited links	a:visited { color: purple; }
:hover	Changes style on hover	a:hover { color: red; }
:active	Styles links when clicked	a:active { color: orange; }
text-decoration	Controls underlining	text-decoration: none;
background-color	Adds background color	background-color: #008CBA;
border-radius	Adds rounded corners	border-radius: 5px;

M. CSS Tables and Layouts

What is CSS Tables and Layouts?

Tables are useful for displaying structured data in rows and columns. With CSS, you can enhance tables by styling borders, spacing, alignment, and even making them responsive for different screen sizes.

Styling Table Borders, Padding, and Alignment

1. Adding Borders to Tables

By default, tables have no borders. You can add and style them using CSS.

Example: Basic Table with Borders

```
table {
    border-collapse: collapse; /* Merges borders into one */
    width: 100%;
}

th, td {
    border: 1px solid black;
    padding: 10px; /* Adds space inside cells */
    text-align: left; /* Aligns text to the left */
}
```

Best for: Creating clean data tables.

Tip: Use border-collapse: separate; if you want spaced borders instead.

2. Adding Padding for Better Spacing

Padding improves readability by adding space inside cells.

Example: Adding Padding

td, th {

   padding: 15px; /* More space inside cells */

}

Best for: Making table content easier to read.

3. Aligning Table Content

You can align text and numbers horizontally and vertically.

Property	Effect
text-align: left/right/center;	Aligns text horizontally
vertical-align: top/middle/bottom;	Aligns text vertically

Example: Aligning Content

th {

   text-align: center; /* Centers headers */

}

td {

   vertical-align: middle; /* Centers text vertically */

}

Best for: Neatly organizing columns and rows.

Responsive Tables with CSS

1. Making Tables Scrollable (For Small Screens)

Large tables don't fit on small screens. A solution is to add horizontal scrolling.

Example: Scrollable Table

```
.table-container {
    overflow-x: auto; /* Enables horizontal scrolling */
}
```

Best for: Keeping tables readable on mobile devices.

2. Responsive Tables with Flexbox & Grid

Instead of traditional tables, use CSS Grid or Flexbox for a modern layout.

Example: Responsive Table Using Grid

```
.table-grid {
    display: grid;
    grid-template-columns: repeat(auto-fit, minmax(100px, 1fr));
}
```

Best for: Tables that adapt to different screen sizes.

Practice Lab: Styling Tables in CSS

Goal: Style tables with borders, padding, alignment, and make them responsive.

Steps:

1. Create an HTML File (index.html)

```
<!DOCTYPE html>
<html lang="en">
<head>
    <meta charset="UTF-8">
    <meta name="viewport" content="width=device-width, initial-scale=1.0">
```

```
    <title>CSS Table Styling</title>
    <link rel="stylesheet" href="styles.css">
  </head>
  <body>
    <h1>Styled Table</h1>
      <div class="table-container">
      <table>
        <tr>
          <th>Name</th>
          <th>Age</th>
          <th>Country</th>
        </tr>
        <tr>
          <td>Alice</td>
          <td>25</td>
          <td>USA</td>
        </tr>
        <tr>
          <td>Bob</td>
          <td>30</td>
          <td>Canada</td>
        </tr>
      </table>
    </div>
  </body>
</html>
```

2. Create a CSS File (styles.css)

/* Table Styling */

```
table {
    border-collapse: collapse;
    width: 100%;
    max-width: 600px;
    margin: 20px auto;
    background-color: #f9f9f9;
}
th, td {
    border: 1px solid #333;
    padding: 15px;
    text-align: left;
}
/* Make Table Responsive */
.table-container {
    overflow-x: auto;
}
```

3. Open index.html in a Web Browser

Observe the styled table and resize the window to see responsiveness!

Summary

Property	Description	Example
border	Adds borders to table cells	border: 1px solid black;
border-collapse	Merges borders into one	border-collapse: collapse;
padding	Adds space inside table cells	padding: 10px;
text-align	Aligns text horizontally	text-align: center;
vertical-align	Aligns text vertically	vertical-align: middle;
overflow-x	Enables horizontal scrolling	overflow-x: auto;

Miquill Nyle

N. Borders and Outlines in CSS

What is Borders and Outlines in CSS?

Borders and outlines help define **visual boundaries** for elements like buttons, boxes, and images. CSS allows you to **customize** their **style, thickness, color, and shape**.

Different Border Styles and Thickness

1. Basic Border Properties

Property	Description	Example
border-width	Controls thickness	border-width: 2px;
border-style	Defines line type	border-style: solid;
border-color	Sets border color	border-color: blue;

Example: Adding a Border

.box {
    border-width: 3px;
    border-style: solid;
    border-color: black;
}
Best for: Styling boxes, buttons, and images.

72

2. Different Border Styles

CSS supports various border styles:

Style	Example
solid	■ ■ ■ ■
dotted	....
dashed	– – – –
double	‖ ‖ ‖
groove	3D effect
ridge	Inverted 3D
inset	Shadow inward
outset	Shadow outward

Example: Using Different Styles

.solid { border: 3px solid black; }

.dashed { border: 3px dashed red; }

.dotted { border: 3px dotted blue; }

.double { border: 5px double green; }

Best for: Customizing the look of divs, buttons, and containers.

3. Border Thickness

You can set different thicknesses for each side.

Example: Individual Border Thickness

.box {

   border-top: 5px solid red;

   border-right: 3px dashed blue;

   border-bottom: 2px dotted green;

```
    border-left: 4px double black,
}
```

Best for: Unique border effects on UI elements.

Applying Rounded Borders
You can create rounded corners using border-radius.

1. Simple Rounded Corners
Example: Basic Rounded Borders
```
.rounded-box {
    border: 3px solid black;
    border-radius: 10px;
}
```

Best for: Buttons, cards, and boxes.

2. Fully Rounded Elements (Circle and Oval)
Example: Circular and Oval Shapes
```
.circle {
    width: 100px;
    height: 100px;
    border: 3px solid blue;
    border-radius: 50%; /* Makes it a circle */
}

.oval {
    width: 150px;
    height: 80px;
```

```
    border: 3px solid red;
    border-radius: 50px;
}
```

Best for: Profile pictures, buttons, and decorative elements.

3. Customizing Border-Radius for Each Corner

You can adjust each corner separately.

Example: Custom Corners

```
.custom-rounded {
    border: 3px solid black;
    border-radius: 10px 20px 30px 40px;
}
```

Best for: Creating unique UI elements.

Practice Lab: Working with Borders and Outlines

Goal: Learn to apply different border styles and rounded corners.

Steps:

1. Create an HTML File (index.html)

```
<!DOCTYPE html>
<html lang="en"><head>
    <meta charset="UTF-8">
    <meta name="viewport" content="width=device-width, initial-scale=1.0">
    <title>CSS Borders</title>
    <link rel="stylesheet" href="styles.css">
</head><body>
    <h1>CSS Borders and Outlines</h1>
    <h2>1. Different Border Styles</h2>
```

```
<div class="solid">Solid Border</div>
<div class="dashed">Dashed Border</div>
<div class="dotted">Dotted Border</div>
<div class="double">Double Border</div>

<h2>2. Rounded Borders</h2>
<div class="rounded-box">Rounded Box</div>
<div class="circle"></div>
<div class="oval"></div>

</body>
</html>
```

2. Create a CSS File (styles.css)

```
/* General Box Styling */
div {
    width: 200px;
    height: 50px;
    margin: 10px;
    text-align: center;
    line-height: 50px;
    font-weight: bold;
}
/* Border Styles */
.solid { border: 3px solid black; }
.dashed { border: 3px dashed red; }
.dotted { border: 3px dotted blue; }
.double { border: 5px double green; }
/* Rounded Borders */
```

```
.rounded-box {
    border: 3px solid black;
    border-radius: 10px;
}
/* Circle */
.circle {
    width: 100px;
    height: 100px;
    border: 3px solid blue;
    border-radius: 50%;
}
/* Oval */
.oval {
    width: 150px;
    height: 80px;
    border: 3px solid red;
    border-radius: 50px;
}
```

3. Open index.html in a Web Browser

Observe different border styles and rounded corners!

Summary

Property	Description	Example
border	Sets all border properties	border: 2px solid red;
border-width	Controls thickness	border-width: 5px;
border-style	Defines style (solid, dashed, etc.)	border-style: dotted;
border-color	Sets color	border-color: blue;
border-radius	Creates rounded corners	border-radius: 10px;

O. Advanced Border Properties

What is Advanced Border Properties?

CSS provides advanced border techniques for fine-tuning the way borders behave across different elements and layouts. In this section, we'll explore border block & inline usage and how to create multi-border effects.

Border Block and Border Inline Usage

Borders can be applied based on writing directions using logical properties like border-block and border-inline.

Property	Description
border-block	Controls the top and bottom borders (vertical in LTR/RTL layouts)
border-inline	Controls the left and right borders (horizontal in LTR/RTL layouts)

These properties adapt automatically based on text direction (ltr or rtl).

1. Border Block (Vertical Borders)

Example: Using border-block

.block-border {

    border-block: 5px solid blue; /* Adds top and bottom border */

    padding: 10px;

}

Best for: Maintaining consistent vertical spacing in different languages.

2. Border Inline (Horizontal Borders)

Example: Using border-inline

.inline-border {

border-inline: 5px dashed red; /* Adds left and right border */

padding: 10px;

}

Best for: Keeping horizontal alignment consistent.

3. Combining Both for Full Border Control

Example: Using Both Properties

.full-border {

    border-block: 4px solid green;

    border-inline: 4px dotted orange;

}

Best for: Dynamically adjusting borders based on text direction.

Multi-Border Effects

You can create layered border effects using box shadows, outlines, and pseudo-elements.

1. Using Outline for Double Borders

Example: Dual Border Using outline

.double-border {

    border: 4px solid black;

    outline: 3px dashed red;

    padding: 10px;

}

Best for: Creating a dual-border effect without using extra elements.

2. Layered Borders with Box Shadow

You can simulate multiple borders using box-shadow.

Example: Box-Shadow Multi-Border

```
.shadow-border {
    border: 3px solid blue;
    box-shadow: 0 0 0 5px red, 0 0 0 10px green;
    padding: 20px;
}
```

Best for: Modern UI effects without extra HTML elements.

3. Using Pseudo-Elements for Creative Borders

Example: Layered Borders Using ::before

```
.layered-border {
    position: relative;
    border: 3px solid black;
    padding: 20px;
}
```

```
.layered-border::before {
    content: "";
    position: absolute;
    top: -5px; left: -5px; right: -5px; bottom: -5px;
    border: 3px dashed red;
    z-index: -1;
}
```

Best for: Fancy buttons and card designs.

Practice Lab: Advanced Border Properties

Goal: Apply border-block, border-inline, and multi-border effects.

Steps:

1. Create an HTML File (index.html)

```
<!DOCTYPE html>
<html lang="en">
<head>
  <meta charset="UTF-8">
  <meta name="viewport" content="width=device-width, initial-scale=1.0">
  <title>Advanced CSS Borders</title>
  <link rel="stylesheet" href="styles.css">
</head>
<body>

  <h1>Advanced CSS Borders</h1>

  <h2>1. Border Block and Inline</h2>
  <div class="block-border">Border Block</div>
  <div class="inline-border">Border Inline</div>

  <h2>2. Multi-Border Effects</h2>
  <div class="double-border">Double Border</div>
  <div class="shadow-border">Box Shadow Border</div>
  <div class="layered-border">Layered Border</div>

</body>
</html>
```

2. Create a CSS File (styles.css)

```
/* General Box Styling */
div {
    width: 200px;
    height: 50px;
    margin: 10px;
    text-align: center;
    line-height: 50px;
    font-weight: bold;
}

/* Border Block & Inline */
.block-border {
    border-block: 5px solid blue;
    padding: 10px;
}

.inline-border {
    border-inline: 5px dashed red;
    padding: 10px;
}

/* Multi-Border Effects */
.double-border {
    border: 4px solid black;
    outline: 3px dashed red;
    padding: 10px;
}

.shadow-border {
```

```
  border: 3px solid blue;
  box-shadow: 0 0 0 5px red, 0 0 0 10px green;
  padding: 20px;
}

.layered-border {
  position: relative;
  border: 3px solid black;
  padding: 20px;
}

.layered-border::before {
  content: "";
  position: absolute;
  top: -5px; left: -5px; right: -5px; bottom: -5px;
  border: 3px dashed red;
  z-index: -1;
}
```

3. Open index.html in a Web Browser

See border effects in action!

Summary

Property	Description	Example
border-block	Controls top & bottom borders	border-block: 2px solid blue;
border-inline	Controls left & right borders	border-inline: 2px dashed red;
outline	Adds an outline outside the border	outline: 3px dotted green;
box-shadow	Creates multiple border effects	box-shadow: 0 0 0 5px red;
::before / ::after	Adds layered border effects	border: 3px solid black;

P. Margins and Spacing in CSS

Margins in CSS control the spacing around elements, ensuring proper layout structure and readability. Understanding margin collapsing and layout spacing is crucial for creating well-structured web pages.

What is Margins and Spacing in CSS?

When two vertical margins meet, CSS collapses them into a single margin instead of adding them together. This prevents excessive spacing in layouts.

Key Rules of Margin Collapsing:

- Only vertical margins (top & bottom) collapse.
- The larger margin takes effect instead of summing both.
- Works for parent-child and sibling elements.

1. Example: Collapsed Margins Between Two Elements

```
.box1 {
    margin-bottom: 30px;
    background-color: lightblue;
    padding: 10px;
}


.box2 {
    margin-top: 20px;  /* This will collapse with box1's bottom margin */
    background-color: lightcoral;
    padding: 10px;
}
```

```
<div class="box1">Box 1</div>
<div class="box2">Box 2</div>
```

Expected Output: Instead of 30px + 20px = 50px, the final margin will be 30px (larger margin wins).

2. Example: Preventing Margin Collapsing

You can avoid margin collapsing by adding padding or a border.

```
.container {
    padding: 1px;  /* Prevents margin collapse */
    background-color: gray;
}
```

```
<div class="container">
    <div class="box1">Box 1</div>
    <div class="box2">Box 2</div>
</div>
```

Result: Both margins will be applied separately instead of collapsing.

Controlling Layout Spacing with Margins

What is Margin Used For?

Margins help control spacing between elements and create visual separation in layouts.

Miquill Nyle

Property	Description
margin-top	Space above an element
margin-bottom	Space below an element
margin-left	Space on the left side
margin-right	Space on the right side
margin	Shorthand for all margins

1. Example: Individual Margins

.box {

  margin-top: 20px;

  margin-right: 10px;

  margin-bottom: 30px;

  margin-left: 15px;

}

Each side has a different margin value.

2. Example: Shorthand Margins

You can simplify by using one-line shorthand:

.box {

  margin: 20px 10px 30px 15px;

}

Other shorthand variations:

- margin: 20px; → All sides get 20px.
- margin: 20px 10px; → Top-Bottom = 20px, Left-Right = 10px.

3. Example: Centering an Element with auto

To center an element horizontally, use margin: auto;.

.center-box {

```
  width: 200px;
  margin: 0 auto;
  background: lightgreen;
  text-align: center;
}
```

```
<div class="center-box">Centered Box</div>
```

Result: The element is centered inside its parent.

4. Example: Negative Margins

Negative values pull elements closer.

```
.negative-margin {
  margin-top: -10px; /* Moves up */
  margin-left: -20px; /* Moves left */
}
```

Useful for overlapping effects but should be used carefully.

Practice Lab: Working with Margins

Goal: Experiment with margin collapsing and layout spacing.

Steps:

1. Create an HTML File (index.html)

```
<!DOCTYPE html>
<html lang="en">
<head>
  <meta charset="UTF-8">
  <meta name="viewport" content="width=device-width, initial-scale=1.0">
```

```
<title>CSS Margins</title>
<link rel="stylesheet" href="styles.css">
</head><body>
<h1>Understanding CSS Margins</h1>
<h2>1. Margin Collapsing</h2>
<div class="box1">Box 1</div>
<div class="box2">Box 2</div>

<h2>2. Preventing Margin Collapse</h2>
<div class="container">
  <div class="box1">Box 1</div>
  <div class="box2">Box 2</div>
</div>

<h2>3. Centering an Element</h2>
<div class="center-box">I'm Centered</div>

</body></html>
```

2. Create a CSS File (styles.css)
```
/* General Box Styling */
div {
    width: 200px;
    padding: 10px;
    text-align: center;
    font-weight: bold;
}
/* Margin Collapsing */
.box1 {
```

```
    margin-bottom: 30px;
    background-color: lightblue;
}
.box2 {
    margin-top: 20px; /* This will collapse with Box1 */
    background-color: lightcoral;
}
/* Preventing Margin Collapse */
.container {
    padding: 1px; /* Prevents margin collapsing */
    background-color: gray;
}
/* Centering an Element */
.center-box {
    width: 200px;
    margin: 0 auto;
    background: lightgreen;
}
```

3. Open index.html in a Web Browser

See margin effects in action!

Summary

Concept	Description
Margin Collapsing	Merges two touching vertical margins into one
margin	Defines space outside an element
Shorthand Margin	margin: 10px 20px; (Top-Bottom Left-Right)
margin: auto;	Centers block elements horizontally
Negative Margins	Moves elements closer

CSS Challenge: Build Your Personal Portfolio

Overview

Your task is to design and style a complete "Personal Portfolio Website" using only HTML and CSS. This will test your knowledge of:

- CSS Roadmap & Evolution
- CSS Syntax, Selectors, and Specificity
- Typography, Colors, Backgrounds, Borders, and Spacing
- Tables, Images, Responsive Design, and Advanced Styling

Scenario: Imagine you're a web developer showcasing your work. You need to build a fully responsive, beautifully styled portfolio website using CSS best practices.

Step 1: Setup Your Project

1. Create a folder for your project.

2. Inside the folder, create:

- index.html → Main HTML structure
- styles.css → External CSS file

3. Link the CSS file to your HTML:

<link rel="stylesheet" href="styles.css">

Step 2: Build the HTML Structure

Your portfolio website should include:

- Navigation Menu (Home, About, Portfolio, Contact)
- Hero Section (Welcome message, your name, and a call-to-action button)
- About Section (Your bio and an image)
- Portfolio Section (A table listing your projects)

- Contact Form (With styled inputs and buttons)

Example HTML:

```
<header>
  <nav>
    <ul>
      <li><a href="#home">Home</a></li>
      <li><a href="#about">About</a></li>
      <li><a href="#portfolio">Portfolio</a></li>
      <li><a href="#contact">Contact</a></li>
    </ul>
  </nav>
</header>

<section id="home">
  <h1>Welcome to My Portfolio</h1>
  <p>Hi, I'm [Your Name], a front-end developer.</p>
  <button>Learn More</button>
</section>
```

Step 3: Apply CSS Styling

Task 1: Basic CSS Rules & Layout

- Apply CSS rules to structure the page.
- Use CSS Grid or Flexbox for responsive layouts.

Example:

```
body {
  font-family: Arial, sans-serif;
  margin: 0;
  padding: 0;
```

```
    background-color: #f4f4f4;
}
header {
    background: #333;
    color: white;
    padding: 15px 0;
    text-align: center;
}
```

Task 2: Selectors & Specificity

- Use element, class, ID, and attribute selectors.
- Apply pseudo-classes (:hover, :focus, etc.).

Example:

```
button:hover {
    background-color: #007BFF;
    color: white;
}
```

Task 3: Colors & Backgrounds

- Use RGB, HEX, or HSL for colors.
- Add a background image to the hero section.

Example:

```
#home {
    background: url('background.jpg') no-repeat center center/cover;
    height: 100vh;
    text-align: center;
    color: white;
}
```

Task 4: Typography & Text Styling

- Use @font-face or Google Fonts.
- Apply text transformations and shadow effects.

Example:

@import
url('https://fonts.googleapis.com/css2?family=Poppins:wght@300;600&display=s
wap');

h1 {
   font-family: 'Poppins', sans-serif;
   text-shadow: 2px 2px 5px rgba(0,0,0,0.3);
}

Task 5: Borders & Spacing

- Use different border styles.
- Apply margin and padding for spacing.

Example:

img {
   border: 5px solid #007BFF;
   border-radius: 10px;
}

Task 6: Styling Links & Buttons

- Apply hover, active, and visited pseudo-classes.
- Add smooth transitions and effects.

Example:

a:hover {
   color: red;

```
text-decoration: underline;
}
```

Task 7: Responsive Design

- Use relative units (em, rem, %, vw, vh).
- Apply media queries for responsiveness.

Example:

```
@media (max-width: 768px) {
  nav ul {
    flex-direction: column;
  }
}
```

Step 4: Advanced Styling Features

Task 1: Responsive Portfolio Table

- Create a styled table for portfolio projects.

Example:

```
<table>
  <tr>
    <th>Project</th>
    <th>Description</th>
    <th>Technologies</th>
  </tr>
  <tr>
    <td>Website A</td>
    <td>A blog platform</td>
    <td>HTML, CSS, JS</td>
  </tr>
</table>
```

Example CSS:

```
table {
    width: 100%;
    border-collapse: collapse;
}
th, td {
    border: 1px solid black;
    padding: 10px;
}
```

Task 2: Image Styling & Filters

- Add image filters for hover effects.

Example:

```
img:hover {
    filter: grayscale(100%);
}
```

Task 3: Advanced Borders & Multi-Border Effects

Use border-block and border-inline.

Example:

```
.card {
    border-block: 5px solid black;
    border-inline: 3px dotted red;
}
```

Congratulations! *You've now completed your CSS at first glance!*

Book Synopsis

Unlock the **power of CSS** and transform plain HTML into **stunning, interactive, and fully responsive web pages**. *CSS at a first glance: Redefining to enhance front-end website* is an essential handbook for beginners and intermediate developers looking to **understand, implement, and innovate with CSS.**

This book takes you on a **comprehensive journey**, starting with the **fundamentals of CSS** and gradually moving towards **advanced techniques**, ensuring you gain the confidence to design modern, visually appealing websites.

Who Is This Book For?

- Beginners looking for a structured, easy-to-follow introduction to CSS
- Intermediate developers who want to solidify their skills and explore advanced techniques
- Designers aiming to enhance web pages with powerful CSS styling

By the end of this book, you'll be able to craft professional, responsive, and visually stunning websites with confidence.

Are you ready to take your CSS skills to the next level? Start reading today and master the art of web styling!

~Miquill Nyle

www.ingramcontent.com/pod-product-compliance
Lightning Source LLC
LaVergne TN
LVHW012317070326
832902LV00004BA/81